The Dua Journal

By Umeda Islamova

For information about permission to reproduce selections from this book, email salaam@theduajournal.com.

Visit our web site at www.theduajournal.com.

PUBLISHER'S DISCLAIMER

ISBN: 978-0-692-04652-4

FIRST EDITION

DEDICATION

To all seeking.

INTRODUCTION

In the name of Allah, the Most Merciful, the Most Kind.

In a way, it is easier to be a Muslim today than it ever was before. Islamic knowledge, teachings, and translations are readily available. The limited access to information that led us to blindly follow what our parents taught is a thing of the past.

But because our generation is bombarded with information, we are missing the soul-touching spirituality of Islam where we reflect, surrender, and constantly feel Allah's presence. This closeness to Allah can be achieved through dua and gratitude.

Islam is more than a set of recited texts and rituals. Much of it is forming a relationship with Allah. Because many people miss this part, they are left empty, lost, or unfulfilled.

It is in our nature to want to share our hopes and worries with someone near and dear, but our instincts aren't always to share with Allah, the only One who can help us attain our hopes and calm our worries.

We gain the greatest wisdom when we realize that nothing and no one can fill our hearts and souls like Allah Himself. Constantly acknowledging and remembering Allah strengthens our iman, which is the foundation of our religious practice.

Use this journal every day to reflect on and record your personal duas and feelings of gratitude. You will find that the simple act of writing will give you clarity and shift your focus to what matters most. This will dramatically change your mindset and improve the quality of your life.

The sections in this journal are designed to help you check-in with Allah, reflect on your day and its choices, and set a path toward self-improvement. With just a few minutes each day, you are committing to an intentional and fulfilled life.

The Dua Journal is the safe and private space for you to let go of distractions and to-do lists and be present with Allah and your life.

The Prophet ﷺ said:
"Whoever wishes that Allah responds to his dua in times of hardship, then let him increase his dua in times of ease."
al-Tirmidhi 3382

I make dua for...

Dua is an open and informal conversation with Allah. It is a way for us to call on Him at any time, any place, and in any situation. With regular practice, we become more aware of Allah's presence with us in every moment and every day. He becomes more significant in our thought process and day to day experiences.

Through dua, we acknowledge that He listens to us at all times, He hears our thoughts, and He is the source of all our hopes. We acknowledge that we are completely dependent on Allah, which is the bedrock of our belief and the beginning of success.

Here are a few basic principles of making dua:

Make dua at all times. Dua is a conversation with Allah, and you should have it regularly, outside of your prayers and this journal, even when you feel joyful and at peace. Get in the habit of consciously monitoring your thoughts and involving Allah in them.

Make dua for all matters. Nothing is too trivial to ask Allah, and nothing is impossible for Him. Even the smallest action cannot happen unless Allah wills it, and His will can heal even the worst of situations.

Make dua with good intentions. Avoid asking for things that will cause harm. Focus on positivity, kindness, and mercy.

Make dua for matters of this world and the hereafter. There must be a balance between the two. Think both short- and long-term when making your duas.

Make dua for yourself first. Then make dua for your loved ones, the Prophet ﷺ, and the community as a whole. Prophet Muhammad ﷺ would often start his dua with himself first. Avoid getting in the habit of asking others to make dua for you and failing to do one for yourself.

Make dua earnestly. Ask from your core. Really want what you are asking for. Be insistent, sincere, and humble, and visualize having your duas answered.

Make dua with an expectation that Allah will respond to it. Expect only the best from Allah. All things are possible and available with Him. Be confident that Allah will hear you and respond.

Make dua even when they are not answered quickly. Don't be discouraged when Allah delays His response. Be patient and keep making dua.

Make dua and set goals towards achieving them. Choose to work with Allah. Don't expect Him to do all the work. The Prophet ﷺ said, "Trust in Allah, but tie your camel." al-Tirmidhi 2517

"Be thankful to Allah:
whoever gives thanks benefits
his own soul, and as for those
who are thankless—Allah is
self-sufficient, worthy
of all praise."

Quran 31:12

I am grateful for...

Gratitude can be for people, things, events, circumstances, etc.
Gratitude isn't just words. It's a habit of acknowledging blessings and giving thanks for being chosen as recipients. It's an exercise of putting greater value on people, things, events, etc. through imagining life without them. Gratitude is acknowledging that those things didn't have to happen or didn't have to be given to us, but because they were, we've gained in some way. Most importantly, gratitude is the willingness to trace the blessings to their source, to Allah.

Here is how gratitude benefits us:

Gratitude makes you humble. Each of us is blessed in so many ways, most of which we take for granted. Through gratitude, we realize that we did not earn any of our blessings. It is humbling to ponder on the fact that Allah chose to gift each of our blessings specifically to us.

Gratitude opens your eyes to your gifts. What if we made a conscious choice to take nothing in our lives for granted, not even the simplest blessings – breathing, our senses, mobility, speech, family, etc.? The more blessings you open your eyes to, the more you will see.

Gratitude increases your patience. It gives us something to hold on to until situations unfold in their proper times.

Gratitude helps you enjoy the now. Our human nature constantly wants more. Gratitude focuses us on what we have by removing the distractions of what we want.

Gratitude helps you recognize the kindness of others. Allah asks us to be grateful to those around us, and to return their favors. Imagine how much better the world would be if people made the choice to make each other happy.

Gratitude increases Allah's blessings upon you. In Surah Ibrahim [14:7], Allah states: "And remember when your Lord proclaimed, 'If you are grateful, I will surely increase you in favor.'"

Gratitude interrupts anxiety, worries, and stress. Practicing gratitude puts our mind on positive things, builds a trusting and loving relationship with Allah, and gives us an understanding that our needs are already being met. Combined, these outcomes keep us away from unproductive, negative emotions.

Gratitude brings contentment. Many scientific studies show that regular practice of gratitude improves physical, mental, and emotional well-being. Gratitude has also been shown to increase positive emotions and improve relationships.

Today's happy moments were...

This is a place to capture positive, joyful moments in your daily life. When you fill out this section, you automatically replay the day's events. It's an enriching experience. Days feel quite short until you stop to reflect on everything they involved. This practice emphasizes everyday happiness that add up to a full life.

Scanning over previous days' entries is an instant mood-lifter as well.

An area I could improve on is... and I will do that by...

There is always room for improvement. This is the space for you to reflect on your behavior and choices which stand between a good day and an even better day. Often, we can control how the day turns out by the way we respond to different situations and circumstances. What is one choice you could have made to make today even better?

Do notice the wording: even better. Be confident that every day is a good day. Every day that you are breathing is a gift from Allah. Every event that you go through is either a blessing or a lesson.

Now think about how you will avoid or make better choices next time. List out steps you will take, things you will avoid, ways you will motivate yourself, and/or how you will be more aware of the tendency so you can manage it better.

Today I learned...

Seeking knowledge is an important aspect of being a Muslim. Knowledge doesn't have to be big. It can be as simple as something you learned about yourself and further reading on current events. Or it can be research related to work, personal life, faith, or hobbies. Be open to learning and make the effort to seek knowledge.

My next level iman goal is...

It doesn't matter where you are in your iman: beginner, intermediate, or expert. It doesn't matter where you were a few years ago either. What matters is that in a few years from now you will be in a higher state. And the only way to ensure that is to take steps today.

There is no 'maintaining' with iman. If you are not taking a step forward, you are surely falling a step back. Don't be overwhelmed though: the steps you take to improve your iman don't have to be big. Focus on incremental improvements: small but continuous.

Perhaps you will schedule ten minutes of Quran reading daily. Perhaps you will aim for consistent Fajr prayers. Perhaps you will spend five more minutes in dua. Perhaps you will take Islamic classes. Perhaps you will attend a Halaqah. You decide what the next small improvement is for you.

Choose what your next small improvement is, for example, praying on time. Then keep writing the same goal over and over until you are praying on time without much effort or reminder. Then move on to the next goal. Aim for consistent progress.

The Prophet ﷺ said:
**"The most beloved
actions to Allah are those
performed consistently,
even if they are few."**
Sahih al-Bukhari 6464

Consistency in reflection

Reading the benefits of dua, gratitude, and reflection are motivating, but it can be difficult to maintain them as regular practices. To reap full benefits, these activities need to be established into habits. Just with forming any other habit, it is a process. Use this journal to stay accountable and consistent.

There are three steps to creating and maintaining a habit:

First, find something you already do consistently, and follow it with The Dua Journal. You might not even recognize these things as habits. They could be picking up your child from school, loading the dishwasher after dinner, working out, brushing your teeth before bed, or, best of all, performing one of your prayers.

As soon as you complete your established habit, grab your journal and find a comfortable place to reflect for a few minutes. Keep your journal in the same place you perform the initial activity (in your car, near the dishwasher, in your workout bag, etc.)

Secondly, don't depend on motivation alone to complete the journal. Motivation comes and goes. You need something more stable to bring about the change you want. Instead, depend on discipline.

Discipline requires persuasion, self-motivation, and becoming your own cheerleader, all to do something you just don't want to do at that moment. Discipline, if you practice it long enough, grows into a habit. Combine discipline and habit, and you get consistency, which is your primary goal.

Third, work hard to never miss more than two consecutive days in your practice. Starting a new journey is hard work. Once you fall off the wagon, it can be just as difficult to restart as it was to take your very first step. So strive to write in your journal as many days in a row as you possibly can.

As with any habit, you will start this journey motivated and determined. At some point, however, writing duas and reflections will feel like a chore. If you follow the steps above and stick through, you'll find your regular practice will completely shift your mindset and perspective. You will find yourself making duas and sharing your gratitude with Allah multiple times throughout the day outside of the journal. This regular interaction with Allah will boost your iman and give you happiness and fulfillment in life.

DATE __ / __ / __

I am starting this journal with an intention to...

_____

_____

_____

_____

_____

_____

_____

_____

_____

_____

_____

_____

_____

_____

_____

_____

_____

_____

_____

_____

_____

_____

_____

_____

_____

_____

DATE __ / __ / __

Start by making dua for every area of your life. I make dua for...

RELIGION & SPIRITUALITY

_____

_____

FAMILY & FRIENDS

_____

_____

HEALTH & WELLNESS

_____

_____

WORK, CAREER & BUSINESS

_____

_____

PERSONAL DEVELOPMENT

_____

_____

WEALTH & FINANCES

_____

_____

FUN & RECREATION

_____

_____

O Allah! Infuse illumination into my heart, my eyes,
my ears, in my muscles, my flesh, my blood, my hair,
my skin, my tongue, and infuse illumination into my life.

I make dua for...

_____

_____

_____

I am grateful for...

_____

_____

_____

Today's happy moments were...

_____

_____

_____

An area I could improve on is... and I will do that by...

_____

Today I learned...

_____

_____

My next level iman goal is...

_____

_____

DATE ___ / ___ / ___

O Allah! Purify my heart from hypocrisy,
my actions from ostentation, my tongue
from lies, and my eyes from treachery.

I make dua for...

_____

_____

_____

I am grateful for...

_____

_____

_____

Today's happy moments were...

_____

_____

_____

An area I could improve on is... and I will do that by...

_____

Today I learned...

_____

_____

My next level iman goal is...

_____

_____

DATE __ / __ / __

O Allah! Scold us not when we forget or make a mistake. Make us not bear that burden for which we have no strength.

I make dua for...

_____

_____

_____

I am grateful for...

_____

_____

_____

Today's happy moments were...

_____

_____

_____

An area I could improve on is... and I will do that by...

_____

Today I learned...

_____

_____

My next level iman goal is...

_____

_____

DATE __ / __ / __

O creator of the heavens and the earth! You alone are my companion in this world and in the hereafter. Cause me to die as a Muslim and include me among the pious.

I make dua for...

_____

_____

_____

I am grateful for...

_____

_____

_____

Today's happy moments were...

_____

_____

_____

An area I could improve on is... and I will do that by...

_____

_____

Today I learned...

_____

_____

My next level iman goal is...

_____

_____

DATE ___ / ___ / ___

O Allah! Increase me in my love for You
and Your Prophet, Muhammad ﷺ.

I make dua for...

_____

_____

_____

I am grateful for...

_____

_____

_____

Today's happy moments were...

_____

_____

_____

An area I could improve on is... and I will do that by...

_____

Today I learned...

_____

_____

My next level iman goal is...

_____

_____

DATE ___ / ___ / ___

O Allah! Please bless me with more opportunities to perform much better worship of You than I have done in the past.

I make dua for...

_____

_____

_____

I am grateful for...

_____

_____

_____

Today's happy moments were...

_____

_____

_____

An area I could improve on is... and I will do that by...

_____

Today I learned...

_____

_____

My next level iman goal is...

_____

_____

O Allah! I ask You for iman that remains forever,
firm guidance and beneficial knowledge.

I make dua for...

_____

_____

_____

I am grateful for...

_____

_____

_____

Today's happy moments were...

_____

_____

_____

An area I could improve on is... and I will do that by...

_____

Today I learned...

_____

_____

My next level iman goal is...

_____

_____

DATE __ / __ / __

O Allah! Forgive us and our brothers who have
preceded us in the faith, and do not put a grudge
in our hearts against those who believe.

I make dua for...

_____

_____

_____

I am grateful for...

_____

_____

_____

Today's happy moments were...

_____

_____

_____

An area I could improve on is... and I will do that by...

_____

Today I learned...

_____

_____

My next level iman goal is...

_____

_____

DATE __ / __ / __

O Allah! I ask You determination like that of the patient ones,
endeavor like that of the fearful, aspiration like that of the
yearning ones, and cognition like that of the knowledgeable.

I make dua for...

_____

_____

_____

I am grateful for...

_____

_____

_____

Today's happy moments were...

_____

_____

_____

An area I could improve on is... and I will do that by...

_____

Today I learned...

_____

_____

My next level iman goal is...

_____

_____

O Allah! I ask You strength for good deeds like that of those who are guided, actions like that of those who have conviction, and sincerity like that of the repentant.

I make dua for...

_____

_____

_____

I am grateful for...

_____

_____

_____

Today's happy moments were...

_____

_____

_____

An area I could improve on is... and I will do that by...

_____

Today I learned...

_____

_____

My next level iman goal is...

_____

_____

DATE __ / __ / __

O Allah! I ask You forgiveness for every good which
I had intended to do solely for You and thereafter
interpolated with something which was not solely for You.

I make dua for...

_____

_____

_____

I am grateful for...

_____

_____

_____

Today's happy moments were...

_____

_____

_____

An area I could improve on is... and I will do that by...

_____

Today I learned...

_____

_____

My next level iman goal is...

_____

_____

26

DATE __ / __ / __

*O Allah! I seek refuge in You from ascribing partners
with You knowingly and I seek refuge in You from
ascribing partners with You unknowingly.*

I make dua for...

_____

_____

_____

I am grateful for...

_____

_____

_____

Today's happy moments were...

_____

_____

_____

An area I could improve on is... and I will do that by...

_____

_____

Today I learned...

_____

_____

My next level iman goal is...

_____

_____

27

DATE __ / __ / __

O Allah! I seek refuge in You from sudden death, from the bite of a snake, from wild animals, from drowning, from getting burnt, and from falling headlong upon something.

I make dua for...

_____
_____
_____

I am grateful for...

_____
_____
_____

Today's happy moments were...

_____
_____
_____

An area I could improve on is... and I will do that by...

_____

Today I learned...

_____
_____

My next level iman goal is...

_____
_____

*All praise is due to Allah who clothed me with which I cover
my shame and with which I beautify myself in my life.*

I make dua for...

_____

_____

_____

I am grateful for...

_____

_____

_____

Today's happy moments were...

_____

_____

_____

An area I could improve on is... and I will do that by...

_____

Today I learned...

_____

_____

My next level iman goal is...

_____

_____

O Allah! Purify our thoughts, purify our intentions,
purify our speech, purify our souls, and purify our hearts.

I make dua for...

_____

_____

_____

I am grateful for...

_____

_____

_____

Today's happy moments were...

_____

_____

_____

An area I could improve on is... and I will do that by...

_____

Today I learned...

_____

_____

My next level iman goal is...

_____

_____

O Allah! Protect me from back-biting, ill-intentions, jealousy, and misunderstandings.

I make dua for...

_____

_____

_____

I am grateful for...

_____

_____

_____

Today's happy moments were...

_____

_____

_____

An area I could improve on is... and I will do that by...

_____

Today I learned...

_____

_____

My next level iman goal is...

_____

_____

DATE __ / __ / __

O Allah! I seek refuge in You from
the trials of the opposite sex.

I make dua for...

_____

_____

_____

I am grateful for...

_____

_____

_____

Today's happy moments were...

_____

_____

_____

An area I could improve on is... and I will do that by...

_____

Today I learned...

_____

_____

My next level iman goal is...

_____

_____

DATE ___ / ___ / ___

O Allah! Make me Yours. Place obedience to
You in my heart. Grant me honor in the eyes
of the people. Save me from evil characteristics.

I make dua for...

_____

_____   .

_____

I am grateful for...

_____

_____

_____

Today's happy moments were...

_____

_____

_____

An area I could improve on is... and I will do that by...

_____

_____

Today I learned...

_____

_____

My next level iman goal is...

_____

_____

DATE ___ / ___ / ___

O Allah! Make the Quran the spring of my heart and the remover of all my sorrow.

I make dua for...

_____

_____

_____

I am grateful for...

_____

_____

_____

Today's happy moments were...

_____

_____

_____

An area I could improve on is... and I will do that by...

_____

Today I learned...

_____

_____

My next level iman goal is...

_____

_____

DATE ___ / ___ / ___

*O Allah! I ask You forgiveness for that sin for which
I had repented to You and then committed it again. I ask You
forgiveness for the promise which I had made then did not fulfill.*

I make dua for...

_____

_____

_____

I am grateful for...

_____

_____

_____

Today's happy moments were...

_____

_____

_____

An area I could improve on is... and I will do that by...

_____

Today I learned...

_____

_____

My next level iman goal is...

_____

_____

DATE ___ / ___ / ___

O Allah! Forgive me for every prayer I had something other than You on my mind, for every time I failed to Praise You, for every moment I could have done more in Your Name and didn't.

I make dua for...

_____

_____

_____

I am grateful for...

_____

_____

_____

Today's happy moments were...

_____

_____

_____

An area I could improve on is... and I will do that by...

_____

Today I learned...

_____

_____

My next level iman goal is...

_____

_____

DATE ___ / ___ / ___

O Allah! Make me an inspiring parent. Help me raise
well-rounded, intelligent, and righteous children.
Control my anger and make me a good listener.

I make dua for...

_____

_____

_____

I am grateful for...

_____

_____

_____

Today's happy moments were...

_____

_____

_____

An area I could improve on is... and I will do that by...

_____

_____

Today I learned...

_____

_____

My next level iman goal is...

_____

_____

DATE __ / __ / __

O Allah! Have mercy on my parents as they brought me up when I was small. Give them wellness, peace, and guidance to the right path.

I make dua for...

_____
_____
_____

I am grateful for...

_____
_____
_____

Today's happy moments were...

_____
_____
_____

An area I could improve on is... and I will do that by...

_____
_____

Today I learned...

_____
_____

My next level iman goal is...

_____
_____

DATE __ / __ / __

O Allah! Make me one who establishes salah and my descendants as well. Accept our supplications.

I make dua for...

_____

_____

_____

I am grateful for...

_____

_____

_____

Today's happy moments were...

_____

_____

_____

An area I could improve on is... and I will do that by...

_____

Today I learned...

_____

_____

My next level iman goal is...

_____

_____

DATE __ / __ / __

O Allah! Motivate me to take care of my health and wellness.
Help me balance all my priorities.

I make dua for...

_____

_____

_____

I am grateful for...

_____

_____

_____

Today's happy moments were...

_____

_____

_____

An area I could improve on is... and I will do that by...

_____

Today I learned...

_____

_____

My next level iman goal is...

_____

_____

DATE __ / __ / __

O Allah! Open up my chest, and make easy for
me my task, and loosen the knot from my tongue,
so that people may fully understand my speech.

I make dua for...

_____

_____

_____

I am grateful for...

_____

_____

_____

Today's happy moments were...

_____

_____

_____

An area I could improve on is... and I will do that by...

_____

_____

Today I learned...

_____

_____

My next level iman goal is...

_____

_____

O Allah! Wash away my sins and purify my heart.
And cause a great distance between me and my sins just
as You caused a great distance between East and West.

I make dua for...

_____

_____

_____

I am grateful for...

_____

_____

_____

Today's happy moments were...

_____

_____

_____

An area I could improve on is... and I will do that by...

_____

_____

Today I learned...

_____

_____

My next level iman goal is...

_____

_____

DATE ___ / ___ / ___

O Allah! Please maintain the peace and security
inside my home, in my community, and in my city.
Give us peace in the world.

I make dua for...

_____

_____

_____

I am grateful for...

_____

_____

_____

Today's happy moments were...

_____

_____

_____

An area I could improve on is... and I will do that by...

_____

Today I learned...

_____

_____

My next level iman goal is...

_____

_____

DATE __ / __ / __

Check in by making dua for each life area. I make dua for...

RELIGION & SPIRITUALITY

_____

_____

FAMILY & FRIENDS

_____

_____

HEALTH & WELLNESS

_____

_____

WORK, CAREER & BUSINESS

_____

_____

PERSONAL DEVELOPMENT

_____

_____

WEALTH & FINANCES

_____

_____

FUN & RECREATION

_____

_____

O Allah! Forgive me, have mercy on me,
grant me peace, and give me sustenance.

I make dua for...

_____

_____

_____

I am grateful for...

_____

_____

_____

Today's happy moments were...

_____

_____

_____

An area I could improve on is... and I will do that by...

_____

_____

Today I learned...

_____

_____

My next level iman goal is...

_____

_____

DATE ___ / ___ / ___ .

O Allah! Forgive me my mistakes, my ignorance, my excesses against myself, and all that You are more aware of than myself.

I make dua for...

_____

_____

_____

I am grateful for...

_____

_____

_____

Today's happy moments were...

_____

_____

_____

An area I could improve on is... and I will do that by...

_____

Today I learned...

_____

_____

My next level iman goal is...

_____

_____

DATE __ / __ / __

*O Allah! I seek refuge in You from lack of courage, from laziness,
from cowardice, from senility, and from debts.*

I I make dua for...

_____

_____

_____

I am grateful for...

_____

_____

_____

Today's happy moments were...

_____

_____

_____

An area I could improve on is... and I will do that by...

_____

_____

Today I learned...

_____

_____

My next level iman goal is...

_____

_____

DATE __ / __ / __

O Allah! Forgive me my sins which I committed intentionally and unintentionally.

I make dua for...

_____

_____

_____

I am grateful for...

_____

_____

_____

Today's happy moments were...

_____

_____

_____

An area I could improve on is... and I will do that by...

_____

Today I learned...

_____

_____

My next level iman goal is...

_____

_____

DATE __ / __ / __

O Allah! Convert our discomfort to comfort, our pains to gains, our tears to smiles, our good dreams to realities.

I make dua for...

_____

_____

_____

I am grateful for...

_____

_____

_____

Today's happy moments were...

_____

_____

_____

An area I could improve on is... and I will do that by...

_____

_____

Today I learned...

_____

_____

My next level iman goal is...

_____

_____

DATE ___ / ___ / ___

O Allah! I ask You for guidance, righteousness, chastity and contentment.

I make dua for...

_____

_____

_____

I am grateful for...

_____

_____

_____

Today's happy moments were...

_____

_____

_____

An area I could improve on is... and I will do that by...

_____

Today I learned...

_____

_____

My next level iman goal is...

_____

_____

O Allah! I ask You for Your love, the love of the person who loves You, and the love of that deed which would draw me closer to Your love.

I make dua for...

_____

_____

_____

I am grateful for...

_____

_____

_____

Today's happy moments were...

_____

_____

_____

An area I could improve on is... and I will do that by...

_____

_____

Today I learned...

_____

_____

My next level iman goal is...

_____

_____

51

DATE ___ / ___ / ___

O Allah! I seek refuge in You from the evil test of poverty,
from the hard-heartedness, from negligence, from destitution,
from humiliation, from distress, and from kufr.

I make dua for...

_____

_____

_____

I am grateful for...

_____

_____

_____

Today's happy moments were...

_____

_____

_____

An area I could improve on is... and I will do that by...

_____

Today I learned...

_____

_____

My next level iman goal is...

_____

_____

DATE ___ / ___ / ___

O Allah! Create love among our hearts, set right our mutual relations, and show us the paths of peace.

I make dua for...

_____

_____

_____

I am grateful for...

_____

_____

_____

Today's happy moments were...

_____

_____

_____

An area I could improve on is... and I will do that by...

_____

Today I learned...

_____

_____

My next level iman goal is...

_____

_____

DATE __ / __ / __

O Allah! I seek refuge from worry, from sorrow, from miserliness, from the domination of people, from that I reach an age of worthlessness, and from the test of the world.

I make dua for...

_____

_____

_____

I am grateful for...

_____

_____

_____

Today's happy moments were...

_____

_____

_____

An area I could improve on is... and I will do that by...

_____

Today I learned...

_____

_____

My next level iman goal is...

_____

_____

DATE ___ / ___ / ___

O Allah! I beg You to bless my hearing, bless my eyesight,
bless my soul, bless my body, bless my manners, bless my family,
bless my life, bless my death, and bless my work.

I make dua for...

_____

_____

_____

I am grateful for...

_____

_____

_____

Today's happy moments were...

_____

_____

_____

An area I could improve on is... and I will do that by...

_____

Today I learned...

_____

_____

My next level iman goal is...

_____

_____

DATE ___ / ___ / ___

O Allah! I ask You for good – all of it –
in the present and in the future, that which
I know of and that which I do not know of.

I make dua for...

_____

_____

_____

I am grateful for...

_____

_____

_____

Today's happy moments were...

_____

_____

_____

An area I could improve on is... and I will do that by...

_____

Today I learned...

_____

_____

My next level iman goal is...

_____

_____

DATE ___ / ___ / ___

O Allah! I ask You for the best questioning,
the best dua, the best success, the best action,
the best reward, the best life and the best death.

I make dua for...

_____

_____

_____

I am grateful for...

_____

_____

_____

Today's happy moments were...

_____

_____

_____

An area I could improve on is... and I will do that by...

_____

_____

Today I learned...

_____

_____

My next level iman goal is...

_____

_____

O Allah! Grant righteousness in my children. Surely,
I have turned to You, and I am of those who have submitted.

I make dua for...

_____

_____

_____

I am grateful for...

_____

_____

_____

Today's happy moments were...

_____

_____

_____

An area I could improve on is... and I will do that by...

_____

_____

Today I learned...

_____

_____

My next level iman goal is...

_____

_____

DATE ___ / ___ / ___

O Allah! Admit those who repented and treaded Your path into paradise which You had promised them, together with the righteous among their forefathers, spouses and children.

I make dua for...

_____

_____

_____

I am grateful for...

_____

_____

_____

Today's happy moments were...

_____

_____

_____

An area I could improve on is... and I will do that by...

_____

_____

Today I learned...

_____

_____

My next level iman goal is...

_____

_____

DATE __ / __ / __

O Allah! Conceal my faults and
change my fear into tranquility.

I make dua for...

_____

_____

_____

I am grateful for...

_____

_____

_____

Today's happy moments were...

_____

_____

_____

An area I could improve on is... and I will do that by...

_____

Today I learned...

_____

_____

My next level iman goal is...

_____

_____

O Allah! I seek refuge from saying things in order to make others hear of it, from doing things for show, from deafness, from dumbness, from madness, and from leprosy.

I make dua for...

I am grateful for...

Today's happy moments were...

An area I could improve on is... and I will do that by...

Today I learned...

My next level iman goal is...

DATE ___ / ___ / ___

O Allah! I ask You pardon and peace in my deen,
in my worldly life, in my family and in my wealth.

I make dua for...

_____

_____

_____

I am grateful for...

_____

_____

_____

Today's happy moments were...

_____

_____

_____

An area I could improve on is... and I will do that by...

_____

Today I learned...

_____

_____

My next level iman goal is...

_____

_____

DATE ___ / ___ / ___

O Allah! Help me against these
mischievous, unjust, and corrupt people.

I make dua for...

_____

_____

_____

I am grateful for...

_____

_____

_____

Today's happy moments were...

_____

_____

_____

An area I could improve on is... and I will do that by...

_____

Today I learned...

_____

_____

My next level iman goal is...

_____

_____

DATE __ / __ / __

*O Allah! I seek refuge from knowledge which is of no benefit,
from a heart which is not submissive, from a soul which is not
satisfied, and from a dua which is not answered.*

I make dua for...

_____

_____

_____

I am grateful for...

_____

_____

_____

Today's happy moments were...

_____

_____

_____

An area I could improve on is... and I will do that by...

_____

Today I learned...

_____

_____

My next level iman goal is...

_____

_____

O Allah! I ask You for an honest tongue, a sound heart and upright character. I ask You for all the good which You have knowledge of and forgiveness for my seen and unseen sins.

I make dua for...

_____

_____

_____

I am grateful for...

_____

_____

_____

Today's happy moments were...

_____

_____

_____

An area I could improve on is... and I will do that by...

_____

_____

Today I learned...

_____

_____

My next level iman goal is...

_____

_____

DATE __ / __ / __

O Allah! I seek refuge with You from loneliness and abandonment.
Surround me with people who will increase my iman.

I make dua for...

_____

_____

_____

I am grateful for...

_____

_____

_____

Today's happy moments were...

_____

_____

_____

An area I could improve on is... and I will do that by...

_____

_____

Today I learned...

_____

_____

My next level iman goal is...

_____

_____

DATE __ / __ / __

O Allah! Please bring me out of the darkness of doubt and favor me with the light of comprehension. Unfold for us the treasure of Your knowledge by Your mercy.

I make dua for...

_____

_____

_____

I am grateful for...

_____

_____

_____

Today's happy moments were...

_____

_____

_____

An area I could improve on is... and I will do that by...

_____

_____

Today I learned...

_____

_____

My next level iman goal is...

_____

_____

DATE __ / __ / __

O Allah! Give me eyes that see the best in people,
a heart that forgives the worst, a mind that forgets
the bad, and a soul that never loses faith.

I make dua for...

_____

_____

_____

I am grateful for...

_____

_____

_____

Today's happy moments were...

_____

_____

_____

An area I could improve on is... and I will do that by...

_____

Today I learned...

_____

_____

My next level iman goal is...

_____

_____

*O Allah! Accept my good deeds. I beg You to
put me on the highest level in Heaven.*

I make dua for...

_____

_____

_____

I am grateful for...

_____

_____

_____

Today's happy moments were...

_____

_____

_____

An area I could improve on is... and I will do that by...

_____

_____

Today I learned...

_____

_____

My next level iman goal is...

_____

_____

O Allah! You have created my soul and You take it back.
Unto You is its death and its life. If You give it life then
protect it, and if You cause it to die, then forgive it.

I make dua for...

_____

_____

_____

I am grateful for...

_____

_____

_____

Today's happy moments were...

_____

_____

_____

An area I could improve on is... and I will do that by...

_____

_____

Today I learned...

_____

_____

My next level iman goal is...

_____

_____

O Allah! I seek refuge in You from every companion who would harm me.

I make dua for...

_____

_____

_____

I am grateful for...

_____

_____

_____

Today's happy moments were...

_____

_____

_____

An area I could improve on is... and I will do that by...

_____

Today I learned...

_____

_____

My next level iman goal is...

_____

_____

O Allah! I seek refuge in You from a worrisome death and I seek refuge in You from a sorrowful death.

I make dua for...

_____

_____

_____

I am grateful for...

_____

_____

_____

Today's happy moments were...

_____

_____

_____

An area I could improve on is... and I will do that by...

_____

_____

Today I learned...

_____

_____

My next level iman goal is...

_____

_____

DATE ___ / ___ / ___

Check in by making dua for each life area. I make dua for...

RELIGION & SPIRITUALITY

_____

_____

FAMILY & FRIENDS

_____

_____

HEALTH & WELLNESS

_____

_____

WORK, CAREER & BUSINESS

_____

_____

PERSONAL DEVELOPMENT

_____

_____

WEALTH & FINANCES

_____

_____

FUN & RECREATION

_____

_____

DATE __ / __ / __

O Allah! I seek refuge in You from having doubts in the truth after having conviction in it. I seek refuge in You from the difficulties of the day of recompense.

I make dua for...

_____

_____

_____

I am grateful for...

_____

_____

_____

Today's happy moments were...

_____

_____

_____

An area I could improve on is... and I will do that by...

_____

_____

Today I learned...

_____

_____

My next level iman goal is...

_____

_____

DATE __ / __ / __

O Allah! I ask You for iman which remains forever. I ask You for a fearing heart. I ask You for true conviction. I ask You for firm religion. I ask You for peace from every calamity.

I make dua for...

_____

_____

_____

I am grateful for...

_____

_____

_____

Today's happy moments were...

_____

_____

_____

An area I could improve on is... and I will do that by...

_____

_____

Today I learned...

_____

_____

My next level iman goal is...

_____

_____

O Allah! I seek refuge in You from intense poverty and extreme need. I seek refuge in You from every poverty which would cause me to become forgetful of You.

I make dua for...

_____

_____

_____

I am grateful for...

_____

_____

_____

Today's happy moments were...

_____

_____

_____

An area I could improve on is... and I will do that by...

_____

_____

Today I learned...

_____

_____

My next level iman goal is...

_____

_____

O Allah! I ask You for a soul which is satisfied with You,
which has conviction in meeting You, which remains happy
with Your commands, and which is satisfied with Your gifts.

I make dua for...

_____

_____

_____

I am grateful for...

_____

_____

_____

Today's happy moments were...

_____

_____

_____

An area I could improve on is... and I will do that by...

_____

_____

Today I learned...

_____

_____

My next level iman goal is...

_____

_____

O Allah! Protect me from chronic illnesses and from long-term dependence on anyone but You.

I make dua for...

_____

_____

_____

I am grateful for...

_____

_____

_____

Today's happy moments were...

_____

_____

_____

An area I could improve on is... and I will do that by...

_____

_____

Today I learned...

_____

_____

My next level iman goal is...

_____

_____

O Allah! Turn the whisperings of my heart into Your fear and Your remembrance. Utilize my courage and desire for that which You love and are pleased with.

I make dua for...

_____

_____

_____

I am grateful for...

_____

_____

_____

Today's happy moments were...

_____

_____

_____

An area I could improve on is... and I will do that by...

_____

_____

Today I learned...

_____

_____

My next level iman goal is...

_____

_____

O Allah! Whenever You test me with regard to anything, be it easy or difficult, keep me steadfast on the true path.

I make dua for...

_____

_____

_____

I am grateful for...

_____

_____

_____

Today's happy moments were...

_____

_____

_____

An area I could improve on is... and I will do that by...

_____

Today I learned...

_____

_____

My next level iman goal is...

_____

_____

O Allah! Make us of Your chosen servants –
whose faces and limbs will be radiant,
who shall be Your honored guests.

I make dua for...

_____

_____

_____

I am grateful for...

_____

_____

_____

Today's happy moments were...

_____

_____

_____

An area I could improve on is... and I will do that by...

_____

Today I learned...

_____

_____

My next level iman goal is...

_____

_____

O Allah! Endow me with the ability to recite Your Book in a manner that would cause You to be pleased with me.

I make dua for...

_____

_____

_____

I am grateful for...

_____

_____

_____

Today's happy moments were...

_____

_____

_____

An area I could improve on is... and I will do that by...

_____

Today I learned...

_____

_____

My next level iman goal is...

_____

_____

O Allah! Help me focus during my prayers. Make my mind present and my words intentional. Protect me from rushing. Make it so I enjoy and look forward to my prayers.

I make dua for...

_____

_____

_____

I am grateful for...

_____

_____

_____

Today's happy moments were...

_____

_____

_____

An area I could improve on is... and I will do that by...

_____

_____

Today I learned...

_____

_____

My next level iman goal is...

_____

_____

DATE ___ / ___ / ___

O Allah! Have mercy on me that I do not unnecessarily do things that are of no benefit to me. Bestow me with good sight in doing deeds that would cause You to be pleased.

I make dua for...

_____

_____

_____

I am grateful for...

_____

_____

_____

Today's happy moments were...

_____

_____

_____

An area I could improve on is... and I will do that by...

_____

_____

Today I learned...

_____

_____

My next level iman goal is...

_____

_____

DATE ___ / ___ / ___

O Allah! Make me, my family and this ummah
both intellectually and emotionally intelligent.
Make us wise and our speech eloquent.

I make dua for...

_____

_____

_____

I am grateful for...

_____

_____

_____

Today's happy moments were...

_____

_____

_____

An area I could improve on is... and I will do that by...

_____

Today I learned...

_____

_____

My next level iman goal is...

_____

_____

O Allah! Forgive me, my parents, and the believers on the day when the reckoning of deeds will take place.

I make dua for...

_____

_____

_____

I am grateful for...

_____

_____

_____

Today's happy moments were...

_____

_____

_____

An area I could improve on is... and I will do that by...

_____

Today I learned...

_____

_____

My next level iman goal is...

_____

_____

DATE ___ / ___ / ___

O Allah! Control my nafs. Protect me from
over-eating, emotional-eating, and binge-eating.

I make dua for...

_____

_____

_____

I am grateful for...

_____

_____

_____

Today's happy moments were...

_____

_____

_____

An area I could improve on is... and I will do that by...

_____

Today I learned...

_____

_____

My next level iman goal is...

_____

_____

DATE __ / __ / __

O Allah! Cause me to enter upon whatever I may do in a manner true and sincere and cause me to leave it in a manner true and sincere, and grant me sustaining strength.

I make dua for...

_____

_____

_____

I am grateful for...

_____

_____

_____

Today's happy moments were...

_____

_____

_____

An area I could improve on is... and I will do that by...

_____

Today I learned...

_____

_____

My next level iman goal is...

_____

_____

O Allah! Grant that our spouses and our offspring be a joy to our eyes, and make us the leaders of the pious.

I make dua for...

_____

_____

_____

I am grateful for...

_____

_____

_____

Today's happy moments were...

_____

_____

_____

An area I could improve on is... and I will do that by...

_____

_____

Today I learned...

_____

_____

My next level iman goal is...

_____

_____

DATE __ / __ / __

O Allah! Give me sufficient energy to carry out
all my duties, both worldly and Islamic duties.
Make me a well-balanced person.

I make dua for...

_____

_____

_____

I am grateful for...

_____

_____

_____

Today's happy moments were...

_____

_____

_____

An area I could improve on is... and I will do that by...

_____

Today I learned...

_____

_____

My next level iman goal is...

_____

_____

DATE ___ / ___ / ___

*O Allah! Inspire me that I may be grateful for the favors
which You bestowed upon me and upon my parents,
and that I may do good deeds which please You.*

I make dua for...

_____

_____

_____

I am grateful for...

_____

_____

_____

Today's happy moments were...

_____

_____

_____

An area I could improve on is... and I will do that by...

_____

_____

Today I learned...

_____

_____

My next level iman goal is...

_____

_____

DATE ___ / ___ / ___

O Allah! Make Your love be more beloved
to me than myself, my family, and more
beloved than cold water on a hot day.

I make dua for...

_____

_____

_____

I am grateful for...

_____

_____

_____

Today's happy moments were...

_____

_____

_____

An area I could improve on is... and I will do that by...

_____

Today I learned...

_____

_____

My next level iman goal is...

_____

_____

DATE ___ / ___ / ___

O Allah! Give to my soul its piety and purify it.
If You see me getting farther away from You,
return me to You in a beautiful way.

I make dua for...

_____

_____

_____

I am grateful for...

_____

_____

_____

Today's happy moments were...

_____

_____

_____

An area I could improve on is... and I will do that by...

_____

Today I learned...

_____

_____

My next level iman goal is...

_____

_____

O Allah! I seek refuge in You from an ill-fated age and from the trials of the chest. I seek refuge in Your honor - there is none worthy of worship but You - that You lead me astray.

I make dua for...

_____

_____

_____

I am grateful for...

_____

_____

_____

Today's happy moments were...

_____

_____

_____

An area I could improve on is... and I will do that by...

_____

Today I learned...

_____

_____

My next level iman goal is...

_____

_____

DATE __ / __ / __

O Allah! Remove us from darkness and take us towards light,
keep us away from all shameful deeds, be they external or internal,
give us blessing in our ears, our eyes, and our hearts.

I make dua for...

_____

_____

_____

I am grateful for...

_____

_____

_____

Today's happy moments were...

_____

_____

_____

An area I could improve on is... and I will do that by...

_____

Today I learned...

_____

_____

My next level iman goal is...

_____

_____

*O Allah! I ask You for steadfastness in matters of religion,
and for the highest standard of integrity. I ask You for gratitude
over Your favors to me and excellence in worshiping You.*

I make dua for...

_____

_____

_____

I am grateful for...

_____

_____

_____

Today's happy moments were...

_____

_____

_____

An area I could improve on is... and I will do that by...

_____

_____

Today I learned...

_____

_____

My next level iman goal is...

_____

_____

O Allah! Protect me from over-spending,
emotional-spending, and unnecessary spending.
Stand in between myself and materialism.

I make dua for...

_____

_____

_____

I am grateful for...

_____

_____

_____

Today's happy moments were...

_____

_____

_____

An area I could improve on is... and I will do that by...

_____

_____

Today I learned...

_____

_____

My next level iman goal is...

_____

_____

DATE __ / __ / __

O Allah! Forgive me for all that I did in the
beginning and all that I did at the end, all that
I did in secrecy and all that I did in the open.

I make dua for...

_____

_____

_____

I am grateful for...

_____

_____

_____

Today's happy moments were...

_____

_____

_____

An area I could improve on is... and I will do that by...

_____

_____

Today I learned...

_____

_____

My next level iman goal is...

_____

_____

O Allah! When I am down, remind me that Your love for me is greater than my disappointments and Your plans for me are better than my dreams.

I make dua for...

_____

_____

_____

I am grateful for...

_____

_____

_____

Today's happy moments were...

_____

_____

_____

An area I could improve on is... and I will do that by...

_____

_____

Today I learned...

_____

_____

My next level iman goal is...

_____

_____

DATE ___ / ___ / ___

O Allah! Protect my children from crowds that will guide them away from You as well as me. Bless them with strong conscience.

I make dua for...

_____

_____

_____

I am grateful for...

_____

_____

_____

Today's happy moments were...

_____

_____

_____

An area I could improve on is... and I will do that by...

_____

Today I learned...

_____

_____

My next level iman goal is...

_____

_____

O Allah! Reconcile with love and understanding between our hearts, resolve our broken affairs, and take us out of darkness of falsehood and ignorance to brightness of truth and guidance.

I make dua for...

_____

_____

_____

I am grateful for...

_____

_____

_____

Today's happy moments were...

_____

_____

_____

An area I could improve on is... and I will do that by...

_____

_____

Today I learned...

_____

_____

My next level iman goal is...

_____

_____

DATE __ / __ / __

Check in by making dua for each life area. I make dua for...

RELIGION & SPIRITUALITY

_____

_____

FAMILY & FRIENDS

_____

_____

HEALTH & WELLNESS

_____

_____

WORK, CAREER & BUSINESS

_____

_____

PERSONAL DEVELOPMENT

_____

_____

WEALTH & FINANCES

_____

_____

FUN & RECREATION

_____

_____

O Allah! Help me and do not help anyone against me.
Grant me victory and do not give anyone victory over me. Devise
plans in my favor and do not allow any plans to work against me.

I make dua for...

_____

_____

_____

I am grateful for...

_____

_____

_____

Today's happy moments were...

_____

_____

_____

An area I could improve on is... and I will do that by...

_____

_____

Today I learned...

_____

_____

My next level iman goal is...

_____

_____

DATE __ / __ / __

O Allah! Open the gates of patience
upon us and cause us to die as Muslims.

I make dua for...

_____

_____

_____

I am grateful for...

_____

_____

_____

Today's happy moments were...

_____

_____

_____

An area I could improve on is... and I will do that by...

_____

Today I learned...

_____

_____

My next level iman goal is...

_____

_____

DATE __ / __ / __

O Allah! Guide me and make guidance easy for me.
Help me against those who oppress me.

I make dua for...

_____

_____

_____

I am grateful for...

_____

_____

_____

Today's happy moments were...

_____

_____

_____

An area I could improve on is... and I will do that by...

_____

_____

Today I learned...

_____

_____

My next level iman goal is...

_____

_____

DATE __ / __ / __

O Allah! Make the most expansive of Your sustenance
upon me be at the time of my old age and
when my life is beginning to leave me.

I make dua for...

_____

_____

_____

I am grateful for...

_____

_____

_____

Today's happy moments were...

_____

_____

_____

An area I could improve on is... and I will do that by...

_____

_____

Today I learned...

_____

_____

My next level iman goal is...

_____

_____

DATE __ / __ / __

O the protector of Islam and its people!
Keep me steadfast through Islam until I meet You.

I make dua for...

_____

_____

_____

I am grateful for...

_____

_____

_____

Today's happy moments were...

_____

_____

_____

An area I could improve on is... and I will do that by...

_____

_____

Today I learned...

_____

_____

My next level iman goal is...

_____

_____

O Allah! I seek refuge in You that I oppress or am oppressed, from something falling upon me and crushing me, and from falling upon something and crushing myself.

I make dua for...

_____

_____

_____

I am grateful for...

_____

_____

_____

Today's happy moments were...

_____

_____

_____

An area I could improve on is... and I will do that by...

_____

_____

Today I learned...

_____

_____

My next level iman goal is...

_____

_____

O Allah! Give me sufficiency in Your lawful sustenance
that I may not be in need of Your unlawful sustenance.
Through Your bounty, make me independent of all except You.

I make dua for...

_____

_____

_____

I am grateful for...

_____

_____

_____

Today's happy moments were...

_____

_____

_____

An area I could improve on is... and I will do that by...

_____

Today I learned...

_____

_____

My next level iman goal is...

_____

_____

O Allah! We ask You for hearts which are compassionate, which are humble and which constantly repent in Your cause.

I make dua for...

_____

_____

_____

I am grateful for...

_____

_____

_____

Today's happy moments were...

_____

_____

_____

An area I could improve on is... and I will do that by...

_____

_____

Today I learned...

_____

_____

My next level iman goal is...

_____

_____

DATE __ / __ / __

O Allah! I ask You for contentment with that which You have apportioned to me of livelihood.

I make dua for...

_____

_____

_____

I am grateful for...

_____

_____

Today's happy moments were...

_____

_____

An area I could improve on is... and I will do that by...

_____

Today I learned...

_____

_____

My next level iman goal is...

_____

_____

O Allah! I seek refuge in You from abhorrent manners, actions, desires, and illnesses.

I make dua for...

_____

_____

_____

I am grateful for...

_____

_____

_____

Today's happy moments were...

_____

_____

_____

An area I could improve on is... and I will do that by...

_____

_____

Today I learned...

_____

_____

My next level iman goal is...

_____

_____

DATE ___ / ___ / ___

O Allah! We seek refuge in You from all temptations,
be they external or internal, from an evil day,
an evil night, an evil hour and an evil companion.

I make dua for...

_____

_____

_____

I am grateful for...

_____

_____

_____

Today's happy moments were...

_____

_____

_____

An area I could improve on is... and I will do that by...

_____

Today I learned...

_____

_____

My next level iman goal is...

_____

_____

DATE __ / __ / __

*O Allah! When You give satisfaction to the
people of this world with their world, give me
satisfaction in engaging in Your worship.*

I make dua for...

_____
_____
_____

I am grateful for...

_____
_____
_____

Today's happy moments were...

_____
_____
_____

An area I could improve on is... and I will do that by...

_____
_____

Today I learned...

_____
_____

My next level iman goal is...

_____
_____

114

DATE __ / __ / __

*O Allah! Make Your love the most beloved of things to me
and make Your fear the most fearful of things in my sight.*

I make dua for...

_____

_____

_____

I am grateful for...

_____

_____

_____

Today's happy moments were...

_____

_____

_____

An area I could improve on is... and I will do that by...

_____

_____

Today I learned...

_____

_____

My next level iman goal is...

_____

_____

DATE __ / __ / __

O Allah! I ask You for good health, chastity,
peace, good character, and to be pleased
with what has been destined for me.

I make dua for...

_____

_____

_____

I am grateful for...

_____

_____

_____

Today's happy moments were...

_____

_____

_____

An area I could improve on is... and I will do that by...

_____

_____

Today I learned...

_____

_____

My next level iman goal is...

_____

_____

DATE ___ / ___ / ___

O Allah! I ask You for unexpected good and I
seek refuge in You from unexpected harm.

I make dua for...

_____

_____

_____

I am grateful for...

_____

_____

_____

Today's happy moments were...

_____

_____

_____

An area I could improve on is... and I will do that by...

_____

Today I learned...

_____

_____

My next level iman goal is...

_____

_____

DATE ___ / ___ / ___

O Allah! Let me live a humble person, let me die a humble person, and raise me among the group of humble persons.

I make dua for...

_____

_____

_____

I am grateful for...

_____

_____

_____

Today's happy moments were...

_____

_____

_____

An area I could improve on is... and I will do that by...

_____

Today I learned...

_____

_____

My next level iman goal is...

_____

_____

DATE ___ / ___ / ___

O Allah! Assist me with knowledge, embellish
me with forbearance, dignify me with piety,
and beautify me with peace.

I make dua for...

_____

_____

_____

I am grateful for...

_____

_____

_____

Today's happy moments were...

_____

_____

_____

An area I could improve on is... and I will do that by...

_____

Today I learned...

_____

_____

My next level iman goal is...

_____

_____

DATE __ / __ / __

O Allah! Give me my book of deeds in my right hand.

I make dua for...

_____

_____

_____

I am grateful for...

_____

_____

_____

Today's happy moments were...

_____

_____

_____

An area I could improve on is... and I will do that by...

_____

Today I learned...

_____

_____

My next level iman goal is...

_____

_____

DATE __ / __ / __

O Allah! Just as You bestowed me with that
which I love, make it a source of help to
me in fulfilling all that which You love.

I make dua for...

_____

_____

_____

I am grateful for...

_____

_____

_____

Today's happy moments were...

_____

_____

_____

An area I could improve on is... and I will do that by...

_____

_____

Today I learned...

_____

_____

My next level iman goal is...

_____

_____

DATE __ / __ / __

O Allah! Remove all worry and sorrow from me.

I make dua for...

_____

_____

_____

I am grateful for...

_____

_____

_____

Today's happy moments were...

_____

_____

_____

An area I could improve on is... and I will do that by...

_____

Today I learned...

_____

_____

My next level iman goal is...

_____

_____

O Allah! Assist me in my religion through this world and in my hereafter through piety. Protect all those things of mine which are hidden from me.

I make dua for...

_____

_____

_____

I am grateful for...

_____

_____

_____

Today's happy moments were...

_____

_____

_____

An area I could improve on is... and I will do that by...

_____

_____

Today I learned...

_____

_____

My next level iman goal is...

_____

_____

*O Allah! I seek Your protection just as You protect a
small child. Make me such that I find solace from
You alone, and that I turn my attention to You alone.*

I make dua for...

_____

_____

_____

I am grateful for...

_____

_____

_____

Today's happy moments were...

_____

_____

_____

An area I could improve on is... and I will do that by...

_____

_____

Today I learned...

_____

_____

My next level iman goal is...

_____

_____

O Allah! Make my internal better than my external. And my external good as well. I ask You for good of that which You give to the people, be it of wealth, a partner or children.

I make dua for...

_____

_____

_____

I am grateful for...

_____

_____

_____

Today's happy moments were...

_____

_____

_____

An area I could improve on is... and I will do that by...

_____

Today I learned...

_____

_____

My next level iman goal is...

_____

_____

DATE ___ / ___ / ___

O Allah! Give me the ability to do that which
You love and are pleased with, be it a word,
an act, a deed, an intention or a way.

I make dua for...

_____

_____

_____

I am grateful for...

_____

_____

_____

Today's happy moments were...

_____

_____

_____

An area I could improve on is... and I will do that by...

_____

Today I learned...

_____

_____

My next level iman goal is...

_____

_____

DATE ___ / ___ / ___

O Allah! Protect me from the evil of myself and
give me courage in setting right my affairs.

I make dua for...

_____

_____

_____

I am grateful for...

_____

_____

_____

Today's happy moments were...

_____

_____

_____

An area I could improve on is... and I will do that by...

_____

_____

Today I learned...

_____

_____

My next level iman goal is...

_____

_____

O Allah! Open the locks of our hearts through Your remembrance, complete upon us Your favor, perfect upon us Your grace and make us from among Your righteous servants.

I make dua for...

_____

_____

_____

I am grateful for...

_____

_____

_____

Today's happy moments were...

_____

_____

_____

An area I could improve on is... and I will do that by...

_____

_____

Today I learned...

_____

_____

My next level iman goal is...

_____

_____

O Allah! I ask You for good health accompanied with iman, iman accompanied with good character, success followed by prosperity, and peace, forgiveness and pleasure from You.

I make dua for...

_____

_____

_____

I am grateful for...

_____

_____

_____

Today's happy moments were...

_____

_____

_____

An area I could improve on is... and I will do that by...

_____

_____

Today I learned...

_____

_____

My next level iman goal is...

_____

_____

DATE __ / __ / __

O Allah! Keep me alive as long as You know
that life is better for me, and cause me to die
once You know that death is better for me.

I make dua for...

_____

_____

_____

I am grateful for...

_____

_____

_____

Today's happy moments were...

_____

_____

_____

An area I could improve on is... and I will do that by...

_____

Today I learned...

_____

_____

My next level iman goal is...

_____

_____

O Allah! Embellish us with the beauty of iman and
make us guides who are themselves guided.

I make dua for...

_____

_____

_____

I am grateful for...

_____

_____

_____

Today's happy moments were...

_____

_____

_____

An area I could improve on is... and I will do that by...

_____

_____

Today I learned...

_____

_____

My next level iman goal is...

_____

_____

DATE ___ / ___ / ___

Check in by making dua for each life area. I make dua for...

RELIGION & SPIRITUALITY

_____

_____

FAMILY & FRIENDS

_____

_____

HEALTH & WELLNESS

_____

_____

WORK, CAREER & BUSINESS

_____

_____

PERSONAL DEVELOPMENT

_____

_____

WEALTH & FINANCES

_____

_____

FUN & RECREATION

_____

_____

O Allah! Make me one who is extremely patient and one who is extremely grateful. Make me insignificant in my own eyes but great in the eyes of the people.

I make dua for...

_____

_____

_____

I am grateful for...

_____

_____

_____

Today's happy moments were...

_____

_____

_____

An area I could improve on is... and I will do that by...

_____

Today I learned...

_____

_____

My next level iman goal is...

_____

_____

*O Allah! Do not deprive me of the blessing of what
You have given me, and do not put me into
temptation for that which You have not given me.*

I make dua for...

_____

_____

_____

I am grateful for...

_____

_____

_____

Today's happy moments were...

_____

_____

_____

An area I could improve on is... and I will do that by...

_____

Today I learned...

_____

_____

My next level iman goal is...

_____

_____

O Allah! Remove the anger of my heart and continually save me from trials that would lead me astray as long as You keep me alive.

I make dua for...

_____

_____

_____

I am grateful for...

_____

_____

_____

Today's happy moments were...

_____

_____

_____

An area I could improve on is... and I will do that by...

_____

_____

Today I learned...

_____

_____

My next level iman goal is...

_____

_____

O Allah! Safeguard me from the front, from behind, from the right, from the left, and from above me. I seek refuge with You from being taken unaware from below me.

I make dua for...

_____

_____

_____

I am grateful for...

_____

_____

_____

Today's happy moments were...

_____

_____

_____

An area I could improve on is... and I will do that by...

_____

_____

Today I learned...

_____

_____

My next level iman goal is...

_____

_____

DATE __ / __ / __

O Allah! Make the first portion of this day into
righteousness, the middle portion of it into prosperity,
and the last portion of it into success.

I make dua for...

_____

_____

_____

I am grateful for...

_____

_____

_____

Today's happy moments were...

_____

_____

_____

An area I could improve on is... and I will do that by...

_____

Today I learned...

_____

_____

My next level iman goal is...

_____

_____

137

O Allah! I ask You the direction to that which is good and correct, to have genuine trust in You, and to have good thoughts about You.

I make dua for...

_____

_____

_____

I am grateful for...

_____

_____

_____

Today's happy moments were...

_____

_____

_____

An area I could improve on is... and I will do that by...

_____

Today I learned...

_____

_____

My next level iman goal is...

_____

_____

O Allah! You are the truth, Your promise is true,
hell is true, the Prophets are true, Muhammad ﷺ
is true and resurrection is true.

I make dua for...

_____

_____

_____

I am grateful for...

_____

_____

_____

Today's happy moments were...

_____

_____

_____

An area I could improve on is... and I will do that by...

_____

Today I learned...

_____

_____

My next level iman goal is...

_____

_____

DATE ___ / ___ / ___

O Allah! Increase my iman, give me peace of mind.
I seek refuge in You from affluence which would
cause me to exceed the bounds set by Islam.

I make dua for...

_____

_____

_____

I am grateful for...

_____

_____

_____

Today's happy moments were...

_____

_____

_____

An area I could improve on is... and I will do that by...

_____

_____

Today I learned...

_____

_____

My next level iman goal is...

_____

_____

O Allah! I ask You to show me what is best, through Your knowledge, and I ask You to empower me, through Your power, and I beg You to grant me Your tremendous favor.

I make dua for...

_____

_____

_____

I am grateful for...

_____

_____

_____

Today's happy moments were...

_____

_____

_____

An area I could improve on is... and I will do that by...

_____

_____

Today I learned...

_____

_____

My next level iman goal is...

_____

_____

DATE __ / __ / __

O Allah! Strengthen the love and respect
between my spouse and I. Make us supportive
and understanding of each other.

I make dua for...

_____

_____

_____

I am grateful for...

_____

_____

_____

Today's happy moments were...

_____

_____

_____

An area I could improve on is... and I will do that by...

_____

Today I learned...

_____

_____

My next level iman goal is...

_____

_____

O Allah! Give us a portion of conviction with which You could make insignificant for us the calamities of this world. Let us enjoy the benefits of our ears, eyes, and strength.

I make dua for...

_____

_____

_____

I am grateful for...

_____

_____

_____

Today's happy moments were...

_____

_____

_____

An area I could improve on is... and I will do that by...

_____

_____

Today I learned...

_____

_____

My next level iman goal is...

_____

_____

DATE __ / __ / __

O Allah! Grant me Your love and the love of that person whose love will benefit me by You.

I make dua for...

_____

_____

_____

I am grateful for...

_____

_____

_____

Today's happy moments were...

_____

_____

_____

An area I could improve on is... and I will do that by...

_____

_____

Today I learned...

_____

_____

My next level iman goal is...

_____

_____

DATE __ / __ / __

O Allah! Strengthen my will to follow Your religion and don't let my surroundings distance me from You.

I make dua for...

_____

_____

_____

I am grateful for...

_____

_____

_____

Today's happy moments were...

_____

_____

_____

An area I could improve on is... and I will do that by...

_____

_____

Today I learned...

_____

_____

My next level iman goal is...

_____

_____

DATE __ / __ / __

O Allah! Safeguard me with Islam while I am standing.
Safeguard me with Islam while I am sitting.
Safeguard me with Islam while I am lying down.

I make dua for...

_____

_____

_____

I am grateful for...

_____

_____

_____

Today's happy moments were...

_____

_____

_____

An area I could improve on is... and I will do that by...

_____

_____

Today I learned...

_____

_____

My next level iman goal is...

_____

_____

*O Allah! I ask You for self-sufficiency
and the sufficiency of my associates.*

I make dua for...

_____

_____

_____

I am grateful for...

_____

_____

_____

Today's happy moments were...

_____

_____

_____

An area I could improve on is... and I will do that by...

_____

_____

Today I learned...

_____

_____

My next level iman goal is...

_____

_____

DATE __ / __ / __

*O Allah! Whatever You kept away from me of the things which
I love but were to my detriment, make them a source of freedom for
me so that I may be able to fulfill all that which You love.*

I make dua for...

_____

_____

_____

I am grateful for...

_____

_____

_____

Today's happy moments were...

_____

_____

_____

An area I could improve on is... and I will do that by...

_____

_____

Today I learned...

_____

_____

My next level iman goal is...

_____

_____

DATE ___ / ___ / ___

O Allah! If this undertaking is in the best interests of my religion,
my life in this world, and my life in the hereafter, then make it
possible for me and make it easy for me and then bless me in it.

I make dua for...

_____

_____

_____

I am grateful for...

_____

_____

_____

Today's happy moments were...

_____

_____

_____

An area I could improve on is... and I will do that by...

_____

Today I learned...

_____

_____

My next level iman goal is...

_____

_____

O Allah! Keep me steadfast in my prayers, my charity, and my fasts, provide me the opportunity to complete Hajj, and increase my awareness of my shahada.

I make dua for...

_____

_____

_____

I am grateful for...

_____

_____

_____

Today's happy moments were...

_____

_____

_____

An area I could improve on is... and I will do that by...

_____

_____

Today I learned...

_____

_____

My next level iman goal is...

_____

_____

DATE __ / __ / __

O Allah! Give us more of Your bounties and do not decrease them, give us honor and do not disgrace us, give us abundance and do not deprive us.

I make dua for...

_____

_____

_____

I am grateful for...

_____

_____

_____

Today's happy moments were...

_____

_____

_____

An area I could improve on is... and I will do that by...

_____

_____

Today I learned...

_____

_____

My next level iman goal is...

_____

_____

151

O Allah! I ask You the ability to do good deeds and to abandon evil deeds. Keep me elevated and do not elevate others over me, and please me and be pleased with me.

I make dua for...

_____

_____

_____

I am grateful for...

_____

_____

_____

Today's happy moments were...

_____

_____

_____

An area I could improve on is... and I will do that by...

_____

_____

Today I learned...

_____

_____

My next level iman goal is...

_____

_____

DATE ___ / ___ / ___

*O Allah! I ask You for paradise and all that would draw
me closer to it, be it by word or deed. I ask that all
which You have decided for me be to my betterment.*

I make dua for...

_____

_____

_____

I am grateful for...

_____

_____

_____

Today's happy moments were...

_____

_____

_____

An area I could improve on is... and I will do that by...

_____

Today I learned...

_____

_____

My next level iman goal is...

_____

_____

O Allah! I seek refuge in You from the evil which I committed and the evil which I did not commit, from the evil which I am aware of and from the evil which I am unaware of.

I make dua for...

_____

_____

_____

I am grateful for...

_____

_____

_____

Today's happy moments were...

_____

_____

_____

An area I could improve on is... and I will do that by...

_____

_____

Today I learned...

_____

_____

My next level iman goal is...

_____

_____

O Allah! Keep me steadfast, make heavy my scales wherein my deeds will be weighed, realize my iman, raise my rank, and accept my salah. I ask You for the elevated stages in paradise.

I make dua for...

_____

_____

_____

I am grateful for...

_____

_____

_____

Today's happy moments were...

_____

_____

_____

An area I could improve on is... and I will do that by...

_____

_____

Today I learned...

_____

_____

My next level iman goal is...

_____

_____

DATE __ / __ / __

O Allah! Bestow on us mercy and provide for us
consciousness of what is right in our affairs. I ask You
for eternal peace. I ask You for gratitude for this peace.

I make dua for...

_____

_____

_____

I am grateful for...

_____

_____

_____

Today's happy moments were...

_____

_____

_____

An area I could improve on is... and I will do that by...

_____

Today I learned...

_____

_____

My next level iman goal is...

_____

_____

O Allah! I seek refuge in You from the animal which moves on its stomach, from the animal which moves on two legs, and from the animal which moves on four legs.

I make dua for...

_____

_____

_____

I am grateful for...

_____

_____

Today's happy moments were...

_____

_____

An area I could improve on is... and I will do that by...

_____

Today I learned...

_____

_____

My next level iman goal is...

_____

_____

O Allah! Purify my heart from hypocrisy,
my actions from ostentation, my tongue
from lies, and my eyes from treachery.

I make dua for...

_____

_____

_____

I am grateful for...

_____

_____

_____

Today's happy moments were...

_____

_____

_____

An area I could improve on is... and I will do that by...

_____

_____

Today I learned...

_____

_____

My next level iman goal is...

_____

_____

DATE __ / __ / __

O Allah! I seek refuge in You from a turbulent marriage,
from children who are a cause of evil upon me,
from wealth which is a cause of punishment upon me.

I make dua for...

_____

_____

_____

I am grateful for...

_____

_____

_____

Today's happy moments were...

_____

_____

_____

An area I could improve on is... and I will do that by...

_____

_____

Today I learned...

_____

_____

My next level iman goal is...

_____

_____

DATE __ / __ / __

O Allah! Make lawful my earnings, give me contentment in whatever You provided me, and do not make me quest something which You have turned away from me.

I make dua for...

_____

_____

_____

I am grateful for...

_____

_____

_____

Today's happy moments were...

_____

_____

_____

An area I could improve on is... and I will do that by...

_____

_____

Today I learned...

_____

_____

_____

My next level iman goal is...

_____

_____

DATE ___ / ___ / ___

Check in by making dua for each life area. I make dua for...

RELIGION & SPIRITUALITY

_____

_____

FAMILY & FRIENDS

_____

_____

HEALTH & WELLNESS

_____

_____

WORK, CAREER & BUSINESS

_____

_____

PERSONAL DEVELOPMENT

_____

_____

WEALTH & FINANCES

_____

_____

FUN & RECREATION

_____

_____

O Allah! I ask You for the reward that is given to the grateful persons, hospitality that is showered upon the close servants of Yours, the companionship of the Prophets.

I make dua for...

_____

_____

_____

I am grateful for...

_____

_____

_____

Today's happy moments were...

_____

_____

_____

An area I could improve on is... and I will do that by...

_____

_____

Today I learned...

_____

_____

My next level iman goal is...

_____

_____

O Allah! Protect me from a deceptive friend: looks with love,
but filled with hatred. When he sees any good in me,
he conceals it. When he sees any evil in me, he exposes it.

I make dua for...

_____

_____

_____

I am grateful for...

_____

_____

_____

Today's happy moments were...

_____

_____

_____

An area I could improve on is... and I will do that by...

_____

_____

Today I learned...

_____

_____

My next level iman goal is...

_____

_____

DATE __ / __ / __

O Allah! I ask You for immediate expanse, beautiful patience, abundant sustenance, peace from all calamities, total peace and independence from people.

I make dua for...

_____

_____

_____

I am grateful for...

_____

_____

_____

Today's happy moments were...

_____

_____

_____

An area I could improve on is... and I will do that by...

_____

Today I learned...

_____

_____

My next level iman goal is...

_____

_____

DATE ___ / ___ / ___

O Allah! Bestow upon me the Glorious Quran,
completely infuse it in my flesh, in my blood, in my
hearing, in my seeing, that You make my body act on it.

I make dua for...

_____

_____

_____

I am grateful for...

_____

_____

_____

Today's happy moments were...

_____

_____

_____

An area I could improve on is... and I will do that by...

_____

Today I learned...

_____

_____

My next level iman goal is...

_____

_____

DATE __ / __ / __

O Allah! I seek refuge in You from slipping or from
causing someone else to slip and from acting ignorantly
or allowing someone to act ignorantly towards me.

I make dua for...

_____

_____

_____

I am grateful for...

_____

_____

_____

Today's happy moments were...

_____

_____

_____

An area I could improve on is... and I will do that by...

_____

Today I learned...

_____

_____

My next level iman goal is...

_____

_____

O Allah! Make us of those who love, for the sake of Your love, and those who love You from amongst Your creation.

I make dua for...

_____

_____

_____

I am grateful for...

_____

_____

_____

Today's happy moments were...

_____

_____

_____

An area I could improve on is... and I will do that by...

_____

Today I learned...

_____

_____

My next level iman goal is...

_____

_____

DATE ___ / ___ / ___

O Allah! We seek refuge in You from going astray
and leading others astray as well. Make us the friends
of Your friends and the enemies of Your enemies.

I make dua for...

_____
_____
_____

I am grateful for...

_____
_____
_____

Today's happy moments were...

_____
_____
_____

An area I could improve on is... and I will do that by...

_____

Today I learned...

_____
_____

My next level iman goal is...

_____
_____

DATE __ / __ / __

O Allah! Do not leave me to myself even for the blink of an eye nor snatch away from me the good that You have bestowed upon me.

I make dua for...

_____

_____

_____

I am grateful for...

_____

_____

_____

Today's happy moments were...

_____

_____

_____

An area I could improve on is... and I will do that by...

_____

_____

Today I learned...

_____

_____

My next level iman goal is...

_____

_____

DATE __ / __ / __

O Allah! You have made my physical appearance
beautiful. Now make beautiful my character.

I make dua for...

_____

_____

_____

I am grateful for...

_____

_____

_____

Today's happy moments were...

_____

_____

_____

An area I could improve on is... and I will do that by...

_____

Today I learned...

_____

_____

My next level iman goal is...

_____

_____

O Allah! I seek refuge in You from drowning, from getting burnt, from Satan confusing me at the time of death, and that I die from being stung by a poisonous creature.

I make dua for...

_____

_____

I am grateful for...

_____

_____

Today's happy moments were...

_____

_____

An area I could improve on is... and I will do that by...

_____

Today I learned...

_____

_____

My next level iman goal is...

_____

_____

*O Allah! I ask You for a pure life, a peaceful death, and
a passing away which is neither disgraceful nor dishonorable.*

I make dua for...

_____

_____

_____

I am grateful for...

_____

_____

_____

Today's happy moments were...

_____

_____

_____

An area I could improve on is... and I will do that by...

_____

Today I learned...

_____

_____

My next level iman goal is...

_____

_____

O Allah! Do not give an enemy or an envious person the cause to take malicious pleasure in any mishap which befalls me. I ask You for all good.

I make dua for...

_____

_____

_____

I am grateful for...

_____

_____

_____

Today's happy moments were...

_____

_____

_____

An area I could improve on is... and I will do that by...

_____

_____

Today I learned...

_____

_____

My next level iman goal is...

_____

_____

O Allah! Accept my repentance, remove my sins, accept my supplication, make my tongue speak the truth, give guidance to my heart and remove malice from within my chest.

I make dua for...

_____

_____

_____

I am grateful for...

_____

_____

_____

Today's happy moments were...

_____

_____

_____

An area I could improve on is... and I will do that by...

_____

Today I learned...

_____

_____

My next level iman goal is...

_____

_____

DATE __ / __ / __

O Allah! Guard me through Your eye which never sleeps,
embrace me with Your strength from which no one can be
separated, have mercy on me through the power which
You have over me so that I am not destroyed.

I make dua for...

_____

_____

_____

I am grateful for...

_____

_____

_____

Today's happy moments were...

_____

_____

_____

An area I could improve on is... and I will do that by...

_____

_____

Today I learned...

_____

_____

_____

My next level iman goal is...

_____

_____

O Allah! Make me such that I remember You abundantly, that I am ever grateful to You, that I am ever fearful of You, that I am ever submissive to You, and that I am ever obedient to You.

I make dua for...

_____

_____

_____

I am grateful for...

_____

_____

_____

Today's happy moments were...

_____

_____

_____

An area I could improve on is... and I will do that by...

_____

_____

Today I learned...

_____

_____

My next level iman goal is...

_____

_____

DATE __ / __ / __

O Allah! Grant paradise to my grandparents. Shed light
in their graves. And give them peace in the hereafter.

I make dua for...

_____

_____

_____

I am grateful for...

_____

_____

_____

Today's happy moments were...

_____

_____

_____

An area I could improve on is... and I will do that by...

_____

_____

Today I learned...

_____

_____

My next level iman goal is...

_____

_____

*O Allah! Do not deviate our hearts after having guided us,
and give us Your mercy, surely You alone are the giver.*

I make dua for...

_____

_____

_____

I am grateful for...

_____

_____

_____

Today's happy moments were...

_____

_____

_____

An area I could improve on is... and I will do that by...

_____

Today I learned...

_____

_____

My next level iman goal is...

_____

_____

*O Allah! Keep me from holding grudges
both intentionally and unintentionally.*

I make dua for...

_____

_____

_____

I am grateful for...

_____

_____

_____

Today's happy moments were...

_____

_____

_____

An area I could improve on is... and I will do that by...

_____

_____

Today I learned...

_____

_____

My next level iman goal is...

_____

_____

DATE ___ / ___ / ___

O Allah! Forgive me, my parents, and whoever enters my house as a believer, and forgive all the believing men and believing women.

I make dua for...

_____

_____

_____

I am grateful for...

_____

_____

_____

Today's happy moments were...

_____

_____

_____

An area I could improve on is... and I will do that by...

_____

Today I learned...

_____

_____

My next level iman goal is...

_____

_____

O Allah! Protect me from holding double-standards.
Give me the inclination to judge myself first and
foremost before I look at others.

I make dua for...

_____

_____

_____

I am grateful for...

_____

_____

_____

Today's happy moments were...

_____

_____

_____

An area I could improve on is... and I will do that by...

_____

_____

Today I learned...

_____

_____

My next level iman goal is...

_____

_____

*O Allah! Make life a source of progress in all good,
and make death a source of deliverance from all evil.*

I make dua for...

_____

_____

_____

I am grateful for...

_____

_____

_____

Today's happy moments were...

_____

_____

_____

An area I could improve on is... and I will do that by...

_____

Today I learned...

_____

_____

My next level iman goal is...

_____

_____

DATE __ / __ / __

O Allah! Do not let our religion be cumbersome to us.
Do not make the world our main object, nor the
extent of our knowledge, nor the limit of our desire.

I make dua for...

_____

_____

_____

I am grateful for...

_____

_____

_____

Today's happy moments were...

_____

_____

_____

An area I could improve on is... and I will do that by...

_____

Today I learned...

_____

_____

My next level iman goal is...

_____

_____

183

O Allah! I ask You for iman which does not change,
bounties which do not end, and the company of our Prophet
Muhammad ﷺ in the highest stages of paradise.

I make dua for...

_____

_____

_____

I am grateful for...

_____

_____

_____

Today's happy moments were...

_____

_____

_____

An area I could improve on is... and I will do that by...

_____

Today I learned...

_____

_____

My next level iman goal is...

_____

_____

DATE ___ / ___ / ___

O Allah! Let me derive benefit from the knowledge which You bestowed upon me, and bestow such knowledge upon me which would be beneficial to me.

I make dua for...

_____

_____

_____

I am grateful for...

_____

_____

_____

Today's happy moments were...

_____

_____

_____

An area I could improve on is... and I will do that by...

_____

Today I learned...

_____

_____

My next level iman goal is...

_____

_____

O Allah! I ask You for Your fear when I am concealed
from everyone and when I am in the presence of everyone.
I ask You for sincerity in prosperity and adversity.

I make dua for...

_____

_____

_____

I am grateful for...

_____

_____

_____

Today's happy moments were...

_____

_____

_____

An area I could improve on is... and I will do that by...

_____

Today I learned...

_____

_____

My next level iman goal is...

_____

_____

*O Allah! I ask You for all the good which
Your servant and Prophet ﷺ had asked for.*

I make dua for...

_____

_____

_____

I am grateful for...

_____

_____

_____

Today's happy moments were...

_____

_____

_____

An area I could improve on is... and I will do that by...

_____

_____

Today I learned...

_____

_____

My next level iman goal is...

_____

_____

DATE ___ / ___ / ___

O Allah! I ask You that whatever matter You have decided for me, the outcome of it should be good.

I make dua for...

_____

_____

_____

I am grateful for...

_____

_____

_____

Today's happy moments were...

_____

_____

_____

An area I could improve on is... and I will do that by...

_____

_____

Today I learned...

_____

_____

My next level iman goal is...

_____

_____

DATE __ / __ / __

O Allah! Make the outcome of all our affairs
good and protect us from the disgrace of this
world and the punishment of the hereafter.

I make dua for...

_____

_____

_____

I am grateful for...

_____

_____

_____

Today's happy moments were...

_____

_____

_____

An area I could improve on is... and I will do that by...

_____

_____

Today I learned...

_____

_____

My next level iman goal is...

_____

_____

189

DATE __ / __ / __

O Allah! Do not leave any worry without having removed it,
nor any debt without having fulfilled it, nor any needs of
this world and the hereafter without having fulfilled them.

I make dua for...

_____

_____

_____

I am grateful for...

_____

_____

_____

Today's happy moments were...

_____

_____

_____

An area I could improve on is... and I will do that by...

_____

Today I learned...

_____

_____

My next level iman goal is...

_____

_____

190

DATE ___ / ___ / ___

Check in by making dua for each life area. *I make dua for...*

RELIGION & SPIRITUALITY

_____

_____

FAMILY & FRIENDS

_____

_____

HEALTH & WELLNESS

_____

_____

WORK, CAREER & BUSINESS

_____

_____

PERSONAL DEVELOPMENT

_____

_____

WEALTH & FINANCES

_____

_____

FUN & RECREATION

_____

_____

DATE __ / __ / __

O Allah! Grant me contentment over that which
You have provided me and give me blessings in it.

I make dua for...

_____

_____

_____

I am grateful for...

_____

_____

_____

Today's happy moments were...

_____

_____

_____

An area I could improve on is... and I will do that by...

_____

Today I learned...

_____

_____

My next level iman goal is...

_____

_____

DATE __ / __ / __

O Allah! Assist us in Your remembrance,
in expressing gratitude to You and in worshiping
You in a most beautiful manner.

I make dua for...

_____

_____

_____

I am grateful for...

_____

_____

_____

Today's happy moments were...

_____

_____

_____

An area I could improve on is... and I will do that by...

_____

_____

Today I learned...

_____

_____

My next level iman goal is...

_____

_____

DATE __ / __ / __

O Allah! Make the best of my life the end of it,
the best of my actions the last of them, the best
of my days the day in which I meet You.

I make dua for...

_____

_____

_____

I am grateful for...

_____

_____

_____

Today's happy moments were...

_____

_____

_____

An area I could improve on is... and I will do that by...

_____

_____

Today I learned...

_____

_____

My next level iman goal is...

_____

_____

O Allah! It is through Your mercy that I am seeking help. Set right all my affairs and do not make me dependent on myself even for a single moment.

I make dua for...

_____

_____

_____

I am grateful for...

_____

_____

_____

Today's happy moments were...

_____

_____

_____

An area I could improve on is... and I will do that by...

_____

Today I learned...

_____

_____

My next level iman goal is...

_____

_____

O Allah! Make me of those who repent
excessively and make me of the purified.

I make dua for...

_____

_____

_____

I am grateful for...

_____

_____

_____

Today's happy moments were...

_____

_____

_____

An area I could improve on is... and I will do that by...

_____

Today I learned...

_____

_____

My next level iman goal is...

_____

_____

DATE __ / __ / __

O Allah! Show me the correct path in
the controversial matters of truth.

I make dua for...

_____

_____

_____

I am grateful for...

_____

_____

_____

Today's happy moments were...

_____

_____

_____

An area I could improve on is... and I will do that by...

_____

Today I learned...

_____

_____

My next level iman goal is...

_____

_____

DATE __ / __ / __

O Allah! I ask that You make the glorious Quran
the fountain of my heart, the light of my eyes, the
eliminator of my grief and the remover of my worries.

I make dua for...

_____

_____

_____

I am grateful for...

_____

_____

_____

Today's happy moments were...

_____

_____

_____

An area I could improve on is... and I will do that by...

_____

_____

Today I learned...

_____

_____

My next level iman goal is...

_____

_____

DATE __ / __ / __

O Allah! Open the ears of my heart for Your remembrance,
and supply me with obedience to You and to Your
Messenger ﷺ, and endow me with practice upon Your book.

I make dua for...

_____

_____

_____

I am grateful for...

_____

_____

_____

Today's happy moments were...

_____

_____

_____

An area I could improve on is... and I will do that by...

_____

Today I learned...

_____

_____

My next level iman goal is...

_____

_____

DATE __ / __ / __

O Allah! Be kind to me by easing all difficulties for me.
I ask You for ease and pardon in this world and in the hereafter.
O Allah! pardon me, for surely You are oft-pardoning, kind.

I make dua for...

_____

_____

_____

I am grateful for...

_____

_____

_____

Today's happy moments were...

_____

_____

_____

An area I could improve on is... and I will do that by...

_____

_____

Today I learned...

_____

_____

My next level iman goal is...

_____

_____

DATE __ / __ / __

O Allah! Choose for me what is best for me
and like for me what is best for me.

I make dua for...

_____

_____

_____

I am grateful for...

_____

_____

_____

Today's happy moments were...

_____

_____

_____

An area I could improve on is... and I will do that by...

_____

Today I learned...

_____

_____

My next level iman goal is...

_____

_____

DATE ___ / ___ / ___

O Allah! I ask You for Your special mercy with which You guide my heart, with which You set aright my religion, with which You fulfill my debts, and with which You safeguard all my things.

I make dua for...

_____

_____

_____

I am grateful for...

_____

_____

_____

Today's happy moments were...

_____

_____

_____

An area I could improve on is... and I will do that by...

_____

Today I learned...

_____

_____

My next level iman goal is...

_____

_____

*O Allah! I ask You for Your special mercy with which
You straighten out for me all my affairs, with which You
illuminate my face, and with which You purify my actions.*

I make dua for...

_____

_____

_____

I am grateful for...

_____

_____

_____

Today's happy moments were...

_____

_____

_____

An area I could improve on is... and I will do that by...

_____

Today I learned...

_____

_____

My next level iman goal is...

_____

_____

DATE ___ / ___ / ___

Allah! I ask You for Your special mercy with which You determine for me all my affairs, with which You inspire my guidance, and with which You restore my love.

I make dua for...

_____

_____

_____

I am grateful for...

_____

_____

_____

Today's happy moments were...

_____

_____

_____

An area I could improve on is... and I will do that by...

_____

_____

Today I learned...

_____

_____

My next level iman goal is...

_____

_____

DATE __ / __ / __

O Allah! Make me among those who, when they do good, they are pleased, and when they commit evil, they seek forgiveness.

I make dua for...

_____

_____

_____

I am grateful for...

_____

_____

_____

Today's happy moments were...

_____

_____

_____

An area I could improve on is... and I will do that by...

_____

_____

Today I learned...

_____

_____

My next level iman goal is...

_____

_____

DATE ___ / ___ / ___

O Allah! I ask You for the good which my opinion has failed to accomplish, which my action have been too weak to fulfill, and which my hopes have not reached.

I make dua for...

_____

_____

_____

I am grateful for...

_____

_____

_____

Today's happy moments were...

_____

_____

_____

An area I could improve on is... and I will do that by...

_____

_____

Today I learned...

_____

_____

My next level iman goal is...

_____

_____

O Allah! Infuse illumination to my right, to my left,
behind me, in front of me, above me and below me.
Make my entire being into an illumination.

I make dua for...

_____

_____

_____

I am grateful for...

_____

_____

_____

Today's happy moments were...

_____

_____

_____

An area I could improve on is... and I will do that by...

_____

_____

Today I learned...

_____

_____

My next level iman goal is...

_____

_____

DATE __ / __ / __

What changes have I noticed through this journey of self-reflection?

_____
_____
_____
_____
_____
_____
_____
_____
_____
_____
_____
_____
_____
_____
_____
_____
_____
_____
_____
_____
_____
_____